The Nature Table Series

Garden Flowers

Trevor Terry and Margaret Linton

Evans Brothers Limited

Flowers

Sweet peas

Stocks

Marigolds

Pansies

Lupins

Dahlias

Flowers

Here are some flowers.

We grow flowers in the garden.

Flowers

We grow sweet peas
in the garden.

Sweet peas have a lovely smell.

Sweet peas

We grow stocks in the garden.

Stocks have a lovely smell too.

Stocks

We grow marigolds
in the garden.

Look at
the bright orange flowers.

Marigolds

We grow pansies
in the garden.

Look at all the colours.

Pansies

We grow lupins in the garden.

Some of these flowers are pink.

Lupins

We grow dahlias in the garden.

Some of these flowers are yellow.

Dahlias

Here are some more flowers.

All these beautiful flowers grew from seeds.

Flowers

A Garden Flower Nature Table

Notes for Teachers and Parents

Garden flowers have always held a special place in the minds of teachers, parents and children, and more often than not they form a colourful bond between all three. Parents are pleased to send flowers to school, and teachers are happy to receive them, not only to brighten their classrooms, but also because such offerings from children can be acknowledged in a very personal way.

Flowers may be thought of as complex and highly specialised mechanisms, wonderfully evolved and adapted to propagate their kind, but it is mostly for their beauty and variety that they should find a place in our classrooms and homes. We use them constantly and in so many different ways to brighten our lives. The wonder of it is that from something as visually unremarkable as seeds we can, with a little trouble and attention, produce living things. That we must care for them is an important social lesson.

Garden flowers will find a place on the Nature Table at most times of the year. Properly arranged in attractive containers, as they deserve to be if brought by children, they give body and colour to otherwise less colourful collections, and make the whole aesthetically pleasing.

Some garden flowers can be grown quickly and it is these which should be raised from seed. Although the best show of bloom will inevitably occur during the summer holiday period there should still be a colourful display in September, more especially if weeds have been controlled. These later flowers can be used to enliven Nature Tables in autumn, and they form a natural link with activities which precede the holiday period. Hardy annuals can be sown directly into the prepared soil of garden plots in April and in this way children will have an opportunity to appreciate a complete life cycle. In the case of half-hardy annuals it is probably better to acquire these as seedling plants ready for planting out at the end of May.

The following are examples of annuals which can

be grown to give pleasure and to provide opportunities for observation and related language development:

* Antirrhinum (Snapdragons)
* Asters
  Calendula (Pot marigolds)
  Centaurea (Cornflowers)
  Clarkia
  Cosmos
  Helianthus (Sunflowers)
  Lathyrus (Sweet peas—dwarf varieties)
  Nasturtium
  Nigella (Love-in-a-mist)
* Petunia
* Tagetes (African and French marigolds)

* Half-hardy annuals

Whether or not there is a garden available, there are usually places for standing plant containers out of doors. In schools, these will enrich and enliven entrances, courtyards and the quieter corners of play areas. There is, of course, the question of watering, and thought needs to be given to the holidays when an occasional soaking may be essential.

Biennials such as wallflowers, forget-me-nots, Canterbury bells and sweet-williams, and perennials like chrysanthemums, lupins and Michaelmas daisies, have life cycles which are too long to be appreciated by very young children. Such flowers can be accepted simply for their attractive appearance, since it is only children aged eight upwards who are likely to be able to appreciate their particular significance.

Children are invariably interested in growing things. Their pleasure will be enhanced when the seeds which they have sown produce flowers which will appear on the Nature Table. There will be a dawning of awareness that a seed, when given the right conditions, will first produce a seedling, to be followed in time by a plant which will ultimately bear flowers, in turn to die releasing seeds to start a new generation.

The reading matter in these books is suitable for 4- to 6-year-olds. The text has been carefully planned so that the beginner, with help, and the child who has made some progress in reading, can quickly experience the success of mastering a book. Repetitive phrases and familiar vocabulary give the child confidence, and visual clues to the less well-known words can often be found in the photographs.

Children will have added interest in the books if they can compare the photographs with real objects. This sensory experience leads to increased awareness, closer observation and a desire to communicate, and what could have been meaningless print begins to make sense. In this way, children gradually acquire a store of words which can be recognised by hearing, by sight, and with *understanding based on personal experience*. This building-up of a 'word bank' is a vital aspect of learning to read.

Published by Evans Brothers Limited,
Montague House, Russell Square, London WC1B 5BX

© Trevor Terry, Margaret Linton, 1979

First published 1979

All rights reserved. No part of this publication may be reproduced, stored in a retrieval system, or transmitted in any form or by any means, electronic, mechanical, photocopying, recording or otherwise, without the prior permission of Evans Brothers Limited.

Acknowledgements
Photographs by courtesy of:
The Harry Smith Horticultural Collection, pp. 2, 3, 5, 19
Jarrold Colour Publications, front cover
Trevor Terry, p. 20
Thompson & Morgan (Ipswich) Ltd, pp. 2, 3, 7, 9, 11, 13, 15, 17
Back cover illustration by Ruth Bartlett

Printed in Great Britain by Sackville Press Ltd., Billericay

ISBN 0 237 29223 8   PRA 6287